PROJECT MANAGEMENT IN THE REAL WORLD

Explaining All This Nonsense About Project Management in Plain English

DAVID R. SHOSTAK, PMP

authorHOUSE®

AuthorHouse™
1663 Liberty Drive
Bloomington, IN 47403
www.authorhouse.com
Phone: 1 (800) 839-8640

Published by AuthorHouse 08/23/2017

ISBN: 978-1-5246-9349-7 (sc)
ISBN: 978-1-5246-9348-0 (e)

Library of Congress Control Number: 2017908170

Print information available on the last page.

Any people depicted in stock imagery provided by Thinkstock are models,
and such images are being used for illustrative purposes only.
Certain stock imagery © Thinkstock.

This book is printed on acid-free paper.

Because of the dynamic nature of the Internet, any web addresses or links contained in
this book may have changed since publication and may no longer be valid. The views
expressed in this work are solely those of the author and do not necessarily reflect the
views of the publisher, and the publisher hereby disclaims any responsibility for them.

Acknowledgement

I want to thank my wife, Barbara, for being my chief supporter, editor, and analyst for all the letters and documents I have written over the years, providing guidance on how to handle many hard and weird situations. I also want to thank Mr. Norman Cherry, my high school teacher who guided me into believing engineering would be a good career for me.

I also want to thank the people in my professional world who had the most influence on me: Murray Hoffman for showing me what loyalty is and seeing the best in people; O.C. Mitchell for showing me what makes a good Project Manager, challenging me, and showing me how to improve myself; Al Jicha for taking the time to provide wisdom and guidance; Rudy Trevison for showing me how to talk my way out of most situations; Mike Mouser for showing me new ways to solve hard problems and collaborating to get great results.

Contents

What is this Book All About?

I decided to write this book because of my 40 years in Project Management. Although there are many books on Project Management, I feel that none of them write about the nitty-gritty different aspects and problem that a hardcore Project Manager has to deal with. What really goes on inside the life of a Project Manager? What trials and tribulations do Project Managers need to face? While dealing with a group of people is very hard, knowing how to get the best out of them is even harder. Developing and maintaining key relationships is very hard because everyone has their own individual opinion about what they think should be done.

My objective for this book is to provide information on what it takes to be a superior Project / Program Manager in the real world. This is not necessarily a step-by-step, can-do book such as demonstrating how to make a better Project Plan, but it calls out what things are going to happen in the real world and how you could deal with them. As the Project Manager you need to listen and sift through all the opinions to pick what is best for the Project as you are the boss of the project. This book presents some real life instances of things that have happened in my Project Management life.

This book is designed to make you think about the situations at work that you follow and fall into. You have to really keep your wits about you or you get sidelined, trapped, and put into situations that are hard to get out of and maybe even into bad ethical decisions. I also want you to think about controversy and maybe I want to play with your head a little bit and tweak your mind. I want to suggest some good ideas to use that I have learned. This book deals with real-life situations that you have to deal with as a human being.

Project Manager's Dilemma

- Why the things you didn't do are more important than the things you did.

- No matter how much you do it will never be enough.

My Professional Background

In 1975 I started working for Hughes Aircraft, the Cadillac/Mercedes Benz of the aerospace industry. I worked my way up from Training Engineer to Field Support Engineer to Project Engineer to Senior Project Engineer to Associate Project Manager. I became a full-blown Project Manager in 1982. I worked with the people who invented radar, lasers, laser receivers, satellite communications and the inventors of digital and wireless applications. I was the Project Manager for the first three-foot (one meter) antenna that become DirecTV satellite communication. We needed to put an antenna in the President's plane, and in the B1 and B52 bombers that could be used for communications. Three key engineers in the Antenna Design Department came up with the design. One day my boss called me into his office and said that Hughes Aircraft wanted to spin off commercially the antenna we were designing and working on. And as he said, "put it into everyone's attic." I thought that this was neat as taking aerospace products and going commercial with them was a hot topic. This antenna later became the antenna for DirecTV.

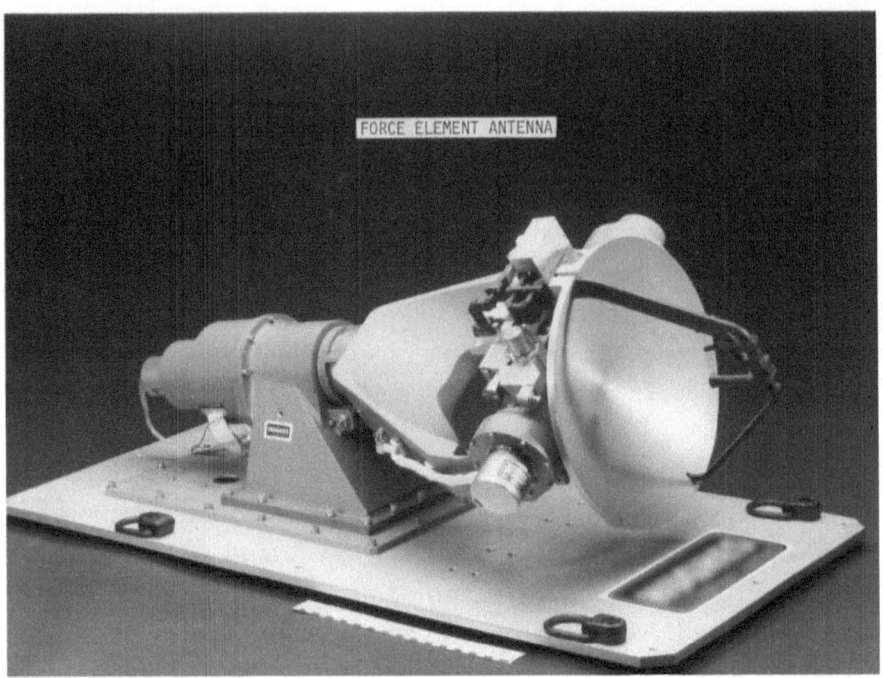

Figure 1 - First DISH TV Antenna Prototype

At this point I decided to go into the commercial world. I landed a job with Magellan as the Project Manager for what we then called the Global Position Satellites (GPS) Low Cost Vehicle Navigation (LCVN). We wanted to make a device/product for GPS Vehicle Navigation in 2003. We were the first company to put a hard drive into the device. Garmin was our main competitor and their vehicle navigation product required users to download the maps from a CD. Our tag line was "Turn it on and go." Magellan gave me two months to plan the project, and, then in January of 2003 we started in earnest. We hired ten new engineers in January and began working on the design on January 10th. Best Buy, the big gorilla of the industry with 650 stores, told us we better have it in their stores by October 17th or we would have a bad Christmas. We had ten months to design, build prototypes, beta test, get to full scale production, and launch the device into Best Buy, Circuit City, and Costco. I led a team of 55 people. We worked through the spring and summer, day and night, and we delivered two days early to Best Buy. What a wonderful feeling!

The toughest part of running this project was dealing with the many personalities on the team. How do you lead a team into battle, knowing that the company was betting its life on the project? In addition, I needed to work with a software development team in Nantes, France, for the European version of the vehicle navigation unit. I also needed to work with the mechanical design group in Taiwan and get the factory set up in China. What worked best was having a very detailed Microsoft Project schedule. I wrote down almost every task that needed to be done and was able to track it. I walked around and talked to everyone. I put together good PowerPoint slide shows for the executives, which my boss help me polish for every presentation. He also let me speak my mind at the meetings. I was able to lay it out on the line and speak plainly. Being from New York City, this was not a hard thing for me to do. I told them what was working and what was not. The senior executives helped me work my way through my problems.

Later in my Program Management life I helped lead an engineering effort to design a GPS semiconductor chip for Nokia cell phones. We got as far as developing limited samples and then we were sold off by RF Micro Devices. But this was a good experience – we learned what it takes to get electronics into a cell phone.

These are three claims to fame I have through my Project Management life. There are a few more.

My Personality

I grew up in New York City and graduated from Pratt Institute with an Electrical Engineering degree. At age 23, I got a job with Hughes Aircraft Company in California and moved from the Big Apple to Los Angeles. After working five years for Hughes Aircraft, I had to make a decision about how I wanted to pursue my career. Did I want to go up the technical ranks or move into management? I decided I was better suited for management so I went up that avenue.

I had a flair for Project Engineering and after two years I was promoted to Senior Project Engineer and then decided to head into Project Management. As a Project Manager I liked getting tasks done. I quickly learned I was headstrong, confident, persistent, and determined because of my New York City upbringing. Yes, I know that sometimes this got in my way. I also learned not to let things get in the way of what you want to accomplish. Life has its hurdles and you need to learn how to get over them. Using my background and developing through trials and tribulations, I honed my New York style, but also learned to be diplomatic. I found that people from California and the Midwest are not accepting of New Yorkers whom they perceive to be pushy and overbearing. It took me a few years to understand this cultural difference and to learn about emotional intelligence. I hope you gain a deep understanding of emotional intelligence from being a Project Manager. Beyond understanding emotional intelligence, the Project Manager must learn how to implement it as a leader. I will use my insights from 40 years of technical Project Management experience with strategy and business management to inspire your leadership capabilities. I have thought a great deal about why people do what they do and why do they do it. When people got in my face, I learned to take a deep breath, and quietly explain what I thought. I also learned you need to pay attention to details. The true understanding of what is going on around you is in the details of the project Scope of Work (SOW) and the Work Breakdown Structure (WBS).

Not a Can-Do Book

What's all this nonsense about Project Management?! Unlike other books that teach the mechanics of Project Management – how to write better Project Charters or Risk Registers or run better meetings - this book presents the real life situations that Project Managers face and the human aspects of projects, such as relationships and negotiating cultural differences. This book will help you understand what it takes to be a superior Project Manager.

Things You need to know

To be at the top of your game as a Project Manager you need to:

1. Be Tough - Be firm and not a pushover.

2. Have a Spine - Stand up and stand your ground to accomplish the objectives of the project.

3. Have Guts - Know when to take the hard risks.

4. Have a Heart - Be diplomatic and soft when you can.

5. Have a Positive Attitude

6. Be Optimistic - See the best in people.

7. Have Desire – Be energetic, have zeal, and get-up-and-go.

8. Have Humility - Bury your ego.

9. Have Fear - Fear is a good motivator to get you to do what needs to get done.

LEADERSHIP
Acronym for Leadership

Here is an acronym I made up for LEADERSHIP:

Long Term Vision
Excellence
Advance Planning
Discipline
Enthusiasm
Responsibility
Sacrifice
Humility
Influence
Perseverance

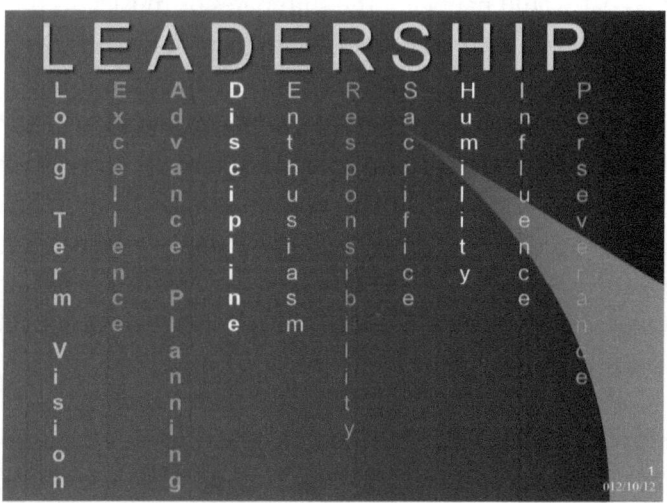

In a matrix organization you may not be the boss of the people on your team, but keep in mind that you are the boss of the project. Sometimes people are fearful of what their boss might say if the Project Manager wants them to do something that will benefit the project, but not necessarily the boss. To take fear away from your teammates, tell them you will take the blame. This means you are strong enough to defend your decision and you know it benefits the project. It also allows your team to breathe, relax, and do a better job. Another thing you can do is go to your teammates' boss and tell him what your teammate(s) need to do. The main thing here is that the success or failure of the project relies in large part on what the Project Manager does. The executives will blame you, the Project Manager, in any event if the project gets into trouble. Also, to some degree the company hired you to successfully manage the project. Succeed with your project and they will forgive many other things you do.

As an engineer and having managed mainly high tech projects, I also know you can make ten technical mistakes, but do not mess with the money or you are dead. Money is the king deliverable in any organization.

So What Does It Take?

Think about it this way; you are the captain of a ship or the conductor of an orchestra. What would happen if the shipmates or musicians did not have a plan or understand their objectives? A Project Manager is the captain of the ship / project in business situations. You need to be tough and persistent. You did not get to where you are by being hesitant or weak-willed. You/they are the ones who have to totally understand and make sense of what needs to be accomplished. What are the true objectives of the project? Think about it this way; you need to take thread and make it into a carpet. You need to deal with hurtles, sand dunes, and obstacles. You are in a major storm with 50-foot waves and 60 m.p.h. winds on the high seas and you are the captain of the ship. How are you going to get the ship into port?

But what if you need to lead a hundred people or even a thousand people on a project? How do you deal with multiple personalities and cultures? You need to be a person that is highly adaptable, willing to be an active listener and worldly about cultural differences. But always, always, keep the objectives of the project in front you and push, push, push...forward.

Remember, you may not be the boss of the people who work with you, but you are the "Boss of the Project."

Project Manager

You need to treat each person as an individual who has different quirks about them. What kind of person are they? What makes up their chemistry? Are they an extrovert or an introvert? Do they just want to be heard? Are they a deep or shallow thinkers? Some talk gobbledygook, but they may be great salespeople. I have found salespeople to be great talkers, but do they actually help your project? If so, make them an ally. How are you going to ally yourself with the Marketing, Public Relations, Finance, Contract, Manufacturing and Sales people?

If you think going to Mars is difficult try dealing with relationships! Or in this case try dealing with a hundred people who are stakeholders with different personalities. Good Luck!

It takes fortitude and determination to get a project through all the major wickets. You have to pay attention to the finer details and maneuver through each one to get to the goal line of finishing a successful project. Each person makes a difference. It's up to you, the Project Manager, to determine how to get the best from each individual to make their contribution to a successful project. They will have a sense of pride when they finish a successful project. This may come on many levels. In the commercial world people actually buy what you made. In aerospace it may be you had produced something that helped win a battle or send a device to the moon or a planet or perhaps the government put it into full-scale production.

Dealing with people is the hardest endeavor you will ever undertake. You need to become a student of emotional intelligence and understand why people do what they do. What fundamental human traits they are following? Do they just want to be heard or vent? Or do they just want to talk to get out something on their mind? Perhaps they are trying to promote their career. Okay! So how do you help them do that? Remember; if they look good or do good, it only helps you and you look good. You also need to have heart for this is what leads to courage - not a closed heart, but an open heart. Heartless leaders don't know how to be open and kind. Having heart and showing you have heart is tough. It's not something you can measure. I also know an open heart will feel pain and that a closed heart won't. Wise leaders know that having a kind heart is essential, especially when leading a group of people and doing tough things. The foundation of extraordinary leadership is heart. The longer I lead, the more I respect leaders with heart - pushing, forcing for results. Pushing for results is ordinary in everyday leadership. But, pushing and forcing for results and having heart at the same timer is what make some leaders extraordinary. The essence of having heart is commitment to connect on a human level with people.

I once had an assistant director at Hughes Aircraft Company who said to me once "David, you need to be a 'Proper Bastard'." Okay, I understood that. He meant you need to be hardnosed at times, keep a strong head, and don't let people sway you from your project objectives. Sometimes you need to stand firm, be diplomatic, and keep the project moving forward. You need to be thick skinned with a Big Heart. Remember, some people want to move their own personal objectives forward, but not necessarily the project objectives.

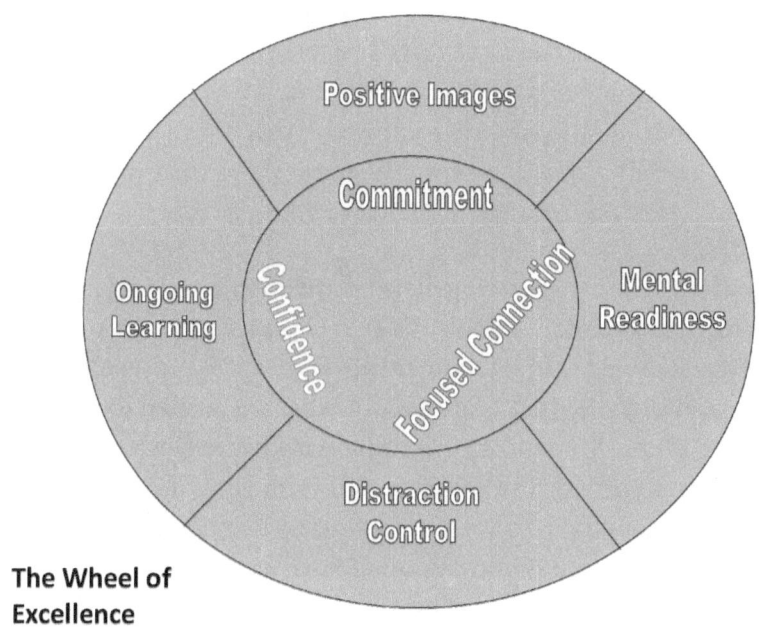

The Wheel of Excellence

Making Plans Reality

"You / I can make a project plan, but it's you / I that has to make it reality." You can make project plans for the ten PMI Knowledge Areas of the Project Management Book of Knowledge (PMBOK) i.e.: Risk, Scope, Time, Communication, Quality, etcetera. But it's you that has to make it become reality. How are you going to get it done? What are your strategy and tactics?

Strategy = a central integrated concept that spells out how we are going to achieve our objectives.

Tactics = What it takes (action) to achieve the objectives.

How will you create and keep a sustainable advantage and capabilities? You need to sit with yourself and figure it out. How are you going to use all your resources to have a successful project? What skills do you have and what skills do you need? Do you have all the hardware and software to accomplish your objectives and goals? What's missing? Who is going to do and be responsible for each task? Do you have enough money and enough time? What are the hard parts and the easy parts of the project? It is one thing to think about what you want to do, but you need to take action to get it done. I would say to myself "yeah, that's a good theory, but can you actually get it done with the money and the time you have? You need to figure out what tactics you are going to use.

For example, when I was at Magellan I developed a strategy to design the GPS for automobiles. It took me two months to do this. We had a Marketing Requirements document to start with and use as a flow down to our design. So first I figured out what we needed to start with in the design phase. System Engineers and Hardware Design Engineers needed to figure this out. The Software and Firmware Engineers needed to figure out what software we were going to use. Then I needed the Software and Hardware Engineers to sit with each other to agree that the software works with the hardware and vice versa. Also we had to keep the Marketing Business Manager involved to let him know how the unit would operate after we had all agreed and bought off on the design.

Then we built prototypes. We needed to make sure they achieved the form, fit, and function of our requirements. We signed up people from the public to test the beta prototypes out on the road, to try them out, and provide feedback every day on what they liked and didn't like, and what worked and didn't work well. I signed up my brother-in-law to be a beta tester in New York City.

Then we needed to make a limited run of production units. Incidentally, a Manufacturing Engineer was part of the team from day one to sit in at the team meetings and provide input on how we would mass produce the Magellan RoadMate GPS vehicle navigation unit. I also had to keep the Public Relations member of the team in the loop to keep the public media informed about what we were doing. I also needed to develop a good quality strategy and configuration management plan. We needed a quality plan to make sure we would environmentally test the unit to meet automotive standards.

So here was my strategy: I stayed informed about each department's progress. I also built up a strong relationship with the Software and Firmware Director. I had a tough time getting the Hardware Manager to provide status and cooperation from his team. They thought the requirements were very tough and they couldn't get them done in time. They thought Marketing had pie-in-the sky requirements. I had to work hard to build up this relationship, but once I did, the Hardware Manager welcomed me into his office and we were able to talk about the project and the hardware progress. Slowly, but surely they achieved their goals.

I also had a tactic of reviewing everything important. I had to sign off on the configuration control documents and on any written material about the Vehicle Navigation device. I also critiqued the manuals included in the box for grammatical errors. In summary, my tactics were that I stayed very close to the project and was able to talk plainly and frankly to the senior executive team which supported my direct and candid responses. My boss was very good at letting me talk plainly to the corporate executive team to get my points across to them. I was able to be honest with my opinions. I once came up with a solution to save $300k in a tooling device, but the CEO wanted to spend the money. This was a bit different to me - that the CEO was willing to spend extra money.

Leadership Criteria to Think About

Leadership Questions from a Trade document:

1. What are your team's aspirations?
2. How do you want people to feel about themselves?
3. How are people finding fulfillment in their responsibilities and roles?
4. How do people know their contribution to organizational mission and vision?

5. What are you doing to develop people?

6. What do you know about your team members' families?

7. What makes your teammates proud?

Words To Live By:

1. Respected

2. Trusted

3. Optimistic

4. Integrity

5. Confident

6. Inspired

7. Challenged

8. Responsible

9. Informed

10. Included

11. Fulfilled

12. Powerful

Words with feelings: How many do you have or show?

1. Spine

2. Guts

3. Attitude

4. Shame

5. Emotion

6. Desire

7. Humiliation

8. Fear

9. Satisfaction

Boss of the Project

Most companies like to use Matrix Management in which the Functional Manager assigns the team members to the Project Manager for the project. During my years as a Project Manager, I have found that people respond better to their boss who holds the purse strings for the project team member's salary and bonuses - their loyalty is to their boss and not as much to you, the Project Manager. Keep in mind, however, and remember that even though the team members come from different departments and you are not their direct boss - **You Are the Boss of The Project.** You are the caretaker and champion of the project. You are the one that has to be sure things get done by the people who are responsible for them. Sometimes team members procrastinate. I have a saying "Don't push the buck to someone else, I asked you to do it!"

Being a Communicator

You need to know how to say the right things, in the right way, in the right place, and at the right time.

People sure communicate in funny ways! We rely on e-mail and voicemail too much and, unfortunately, people don't always read or answer e-mails or voice-mails. I found it was best to get out of my chair and walk to their offices to speak with them face to face. People also don't like to walk to other people's offices especially if they are in another building a hundred yards away. It is worth the effort, however, take the time to talk to the people you need to because it helps you meet your objectives and completes or closes the loop with other people. Simple as it sounds, it also provides the glue to each of the blocks in Project Management.

Communicate, communicate, communicate! Communication is one of the most important things you will ever do. You need to communicate with administration people, staff people, your team, your peers and the executives. Learn how to communicate clearly, to the point and to get your message across. I was always ready to talk to the President or CEO of my company. Often this happened in the elevator at work. I would ask them how their day was going and quickly tell them about my project. It was not always a positive message. I liked to let them know what was going on. Sometimes they offered tidbits on how they could help or who I could talk to. They were always interested in how the project was going because it affects the company's bottom line. The funny thing is I liked to go running at lunch and I would get into the elevator in my running shorts and dri-fit tee shirt. The executives would say how they would like to go run and so I would invite them to join me. It was a light moment in which we both appreciated knowing they would probably not join me, but it broke the ice and they got to know me.

Remember what communication is:

1. Communication is timely and the information appropriate. If it is not, your audience will take it the wrong way and then you may need to do a follow up to clarify what you just said.

2. Plan how to handle the communication. Be clear and practice what you want to say before you say it. Think about your audience and how they will accept the message. If the message is not clear, you may need extra time to explain what you meant.

3. Consider who you are going to distribute the information to. It needs to go to the right set of people.

4. It is important to control and monitor the information as you do not want it going through the wrong channels or to people who can do you harm.

Communication is the most important tool a Project Manager has. You cannot over-communicate. As a Project Manager, I never want to hear or learn from a team member at the end of a project that they were not told or did not hear a critical piece of information. If at the beginning of a project, the team member asked about anything they did not understand, I could resolved it quicker, faster, and better. That is why I always asked my team at the beginning of a project what was in their way and what did they need to make their piece of the project better. What software or hardware did they need? Maybe I can provide it. Through this communication – and by asking – the Project Manager will get to know the constraints the team members may have. Take the hurdles out of their way.

Remember also that communication is a two-way street. Actively listen to the person you are communicating with. Sometimes our minds focus on other things. Try to stay on point and listen to what people are saying. Be a good listener - to all sides of a situation. For example, you might hear from one side of your team that the other side is not supporting them in some way. So you go to the other side to hear their point of view. In this situation I would then get both sides together with me in a friendly environment to go over the issues and work them out peacefully. For example, the Software people could say that the Hardware people are all messed up. When you talk to the Hardware people, they say the Software people are all messed up. What you need is to get the two sides together to talk and work it out.

There are many ways to communicate these days - pick the most effective ones. People do not always read their e-mails. I have a practice of reading every message I get by the end of the day. Sometimes, I received over one hundred e-mails in a single day. I was copied on many of these e-mails for informational purposes and did not need to respond them, but they kept me informed about what was going on. A Project Manager must stay in the game / project and not lose control.

When communicating with people you need to distinguish between what was said and what was meant. There is a difference. Also in our increasingly diverse society, English is not a first language for many people. If it is hard to understand what a person is saying because English is their second (or third) language, tell them nicely that it is hard to understand them, so they can get better at their own communication. Grammatical skill in writing is also important. The lack of a comma or lack of clarity in writing can result in miscommunication or misunderstandings.

Communicating at Major Meetings and PowerPoint Presentations

To demonstrate value and truly understand what is going on at meetings, you need to act as a true performer. Here are a few things you should know:

1. Know the material that you will be presenting. This will show that you are an authority on your project and you understand the whole picture.

2. Speak clearly.

3. Always keep your head-up or in a neutral position when speaking. People see you in a weak position when you look down.

4. Stand with your feet planted on the ground and look tall.

5. Being nervous at the beginning of the meeting is natural. Once you get into the meeting the nervousness will go away.

6. Know the room. Arrive early to your meeting and find out how the room is organized and how you might use the logistics to your advantage.

7. People like it when you over-exaggerate. Exaggeration can help people understand your point or objective better.

8. Use descriptive adjectives. Use the five senses to describe what you are saying. For example:

   a. **Visual:** "I don't see how you get such a distorted picture of that."

   b. **Auditory:** "I hear what you are saying, but it doesn't sound right to me."

   c. **Kinesthetic:** "That doesn't feel right to me! I just can't get a handle on it."

   d. **Taste:** "That situation left a bad taste in my mouth."

   e. **Smell:** "It smells fishy to me."

Holding Meetings and Communicating at Team Meetings

Here are methods to use to get the most out of team meetings and smaller meetings where PowerPoint is not used:

1. Start your meetings on time whether or not all the people are there. This will train people to come to your meetings on time.

2. Also, end your meetings on time. People hate it when meetings run long.

3. Keep your meetings to between 45 minutes and one hour - 30 minutes is even better, if possible.

4. Use an agenda. This is a handy tool to keep the meetings on course and accomplish what you need to accomplish. If someone

talks about a topic that is not on the agenda, stop them. Tell them that since the topic is not on the agenda, we will place it into the "Parking Lot". The last thing on my agenda labeled "Parking Lot". This is where all topics that are not on the agenda are placed; if we have time at the end of the meeting we can talk about Parking Lot topics.

Sample Agenda
LCVN Integrated Project Team Meeting
Low Cost Management Team
Tuesday, April 30th, 2017
4:00 to 4:30 P.M.

Ground Rules:

1. To Review Project Status:

    a. What have you been working on?

    b. Are you on schedule / progressing?

    c. What are the issues and how long do you need to solve them?

    d. What risks do you face (scope creep or scope change?)

    e. What was a success this week?

    f. What are your next steps?

2. Review Action Items

3. Parking Lot Topics (if time permits)

Start Time	Topic	Leader
4:00	Introduction	David
4:02	IC Design	Paul
4:10	System Engineer	Vijay
4:13	Product Engineer	Steve
4:20	Test Engineer	Bryan
4:27	Application Engineer	Kathy
4:29	Package Engineer	CS
4:29	Parking Lot	Et al
4:30	Adjourn	

Getting People to Come on Time to Meetings

Most people do not come on time to meetings. They are a few minutes to 10 minutes late. Using peer pressure is a good way to stop people from coming late.

Bring bagels, donuts, fruit, etc. to your first meeting. Then tell the group that whoever comes in last to the next meeting has to bring the bagels to the following meeting. Use peer pressure to enforce it. People will start showing up at your meetings on time.

Know Thy Self

To communicate well with people, you need to get to know them. And they need to get to know you. You need to understand your own style. Are you direct, casual, or formal? Do you talk loudly or softly? Are you compassionate, empathetic, or non-emotional and like a piece of steel? Do you let others talk without interrupting?

Remember, communication is a mutual process. The more people know about you and who you are, the better the communication will be.

How do you feel about your communication skills? If you think they need improvement, join a Toastmasters Club. Toastmasters helps by giving you feedback in a safe environment. They help you improve your communication and leadership skills. To be an effective Project Manager you must have good communication skills and be able to speak and listen well.

Methods for Controlling Communication

How are you going to control your communication? Remember, good communication has to be both timely and appropriate, so people do not get confused. Otherwise, chaos can occur, which makes the situation even worse.

Team meetings are a good place to disclose necessary information to your core team.

E-mails to people: While e-mails can be effective, they are not always a good way to communicate because people do not always read them. Not only is this inefficient, but you do not know when or if they will respond.

One-on-one meetings are a good way to get to know each person on your team. It is a casual way to get to know them and their style. In this type of meeting, you become acquainted with each other at different levels. You learn what people like and do not like on a personal level. You learn more about their background and who they are, their family situation. Why do this? We do this because the team member gets to know you as a person at a deeper level and not just as a manager or boss. You can see one another as a real person. This can only help you and them. It will help them feel more like a team member.

Spend time around the "water cooler" or just walking around and meeting people in the hallways. It is interesting what you can find out by running into people outside their office or meetings. It works because you meet people in a more relaxed setting, which fosters better communication. I once had a situation where the Software Team Leader told me he needed a piece of software called MathLab. He explained early in the project how this would help the entire project. I was able to get it purchased for him and he was very happy. It helped my creditability as a go-to guy for him.

Stakeholder Needs

Remember, you have stakeholders all around you. Stakeholders range from people who are ancillary in the organization all the way up to chief executives. Sometimes it's interesting what you can find out from the janitor. Remember: "I make a difference, you make a difference, we all make a difference, together we make a difference."

Who are the influencers on your team? They are the ones who have more clout, as well as the Subject Matter Experts. Who impacts your project? Who are the stakeholders outside the project team that have influence or can support positively or negatively? How do you control them?

Play, Learn and Grow Together

Communication Obstacles and Emotions

I am not immune to having someone push my button, getting me very upset and angry. I learned that I get angry if I feel that I am being disrespected, but I also learned being angry creates obstacles to getting things done. I learned to deal with it. I learned to take a deep breath and withdraw or disengage and think about what happened. Do I need to take corrective action? Or do I just let it go and say tomorrow is a new day and you and your team will be better? This is part of having good and strong emotional Intelligence.

I learned to deal with emotions. We are human and get emotional over many things, but keeping our emotions intact and on an even keel helps you move forward with your project and team members.

There are also people who put obstacles in your way. When this happens keep in mind what is best for the project. Remember, you are the boss of the project. Ask people who create obstacles why they are doing it. See if you can persuade them to your side.

Ineffective listening also creates obstacles. Sometimes my mind tunes out what a person is saying because something else is on my mind. I usually end up asking the person to repeat what they said. However, if I actively pay attention and force myself to listen, I get all the information the person is sharing and understand it the first time, and you get answers quicker and more efficiently.

Sometimes there is what I call "noise in the transmission" when someone is talking. Is it the cell phone, telephone, or just the person's speech? Sometimes it is hard to understand what a person is saying, especially if English is not their first language. There can also be noise in the receiving of the information. These things are obstacles to communication. So if you stay sharp, keep your mind awake and open to the situation, you can communicate more effectively with fewer obstacles.

What Are Our Tools When We Communicate?

We are not always aware of the nonverbal tools we use to communicate. Humans use our bodies, our faces, our eyes and our hands when we communicate. These are all tools you need to use masterfully. Use these tools to your advantage to help you get your points across more convincingly. Again, this is where Toastmasters could help you hone your nonverbal skills.

What about your verbal skills - your speech and your voice? They say having a voice in a deeper more bass like in a lower pitch is better to improving your voice. People often leave me voicemails where they talk faster than I can comprehend them. There have been times I have had to listen to the message five times before I understood what they said. I have learned to talk slowly and distinctly when leaving a voicemail, especially when I leave my phone number. Be aware of the volume you use when you speak. Some people speak louder than others. I have a very loud voice. I do not hear myself, but I have learned to talk lower. I try to be conscious of that when I speak. How loud are you when you talk?

Remember, your body language communicates as much as your voice does. Gestures and visual aids make communication better. Your voice and body language together make up the full package and are the best way to go.

Understanding what Project Management is and why

Most companies do not understand what a project manager is and why they are needed. They think teams of people can just do things by themselves and their projects will succeed. Well, let me tell you why Project Management was invented. It was invented in the Aerospace world in the 1950's and 60's. I had the honor of meeting and working for one of the fathers of Project Management, Clair Carlson. Clair was the President of the Ground Systems Group and lead several Divisions of Hughes Aircraft Company where I worked in Fullerton, California.

Clair once told me that he learned that the engineers in the company were a poor fit for talking to customers and they did not understand business principles. Engineers spoke about all their problems and would get the customers worried. Engineers, by definition, are totally honest and have opinions that could scare customers. It is very difficult to achieve all the objectives of an aerospace project. We would say the military desires and wants ten pounds in a five-pound bag. We also used to say that the one thing worse than having a military contract is not having one.

Clair also felt that engineers did not understand how to budget their work. They did not pay attention to the cost of the project. He said he needed people who could lead the project, work well with customers and be responsible for the budget and schedule of the project. Clair invented the Project Manager - someone who could understand the technical aspects of the project, but be a business savvy person as well.

Hughes Aircraft started a school for Project Managers. They would pick only one person per Division to attend the school. It lasted one year. I was honored to be one of them. I beat out some stiff competition from far more senior people. I got to meet the top executives in the company as they would teach the different modules of the syllabus. There were about 20 different modules including such topics as contracts, procurement and system engineering. I received a great understanding of what Project Management is and what it is not from the people who lived and worked major projects and grew into the top executives of the company. This is how I was able to meet Clair and talk with him on a personal level.

What most companies do not understand is what value a good Project Manager brings to the company. The Project Manager is the conductor and director of the project. He is the leader and the one who is going to set the tone of what gets done and what doesn't get done. The Project Manager's value is that he / she will do whatever it takes to make a successful project. If that means doing simple administrative tasks, so be it. I am quite serious when I say I will sweep the floors and wash the bathrooms if I need to. I have been told that I do the job of ten other people for I will do more than what is in my job description. I become a jack-of-all-trades and work to get it done. The good Project Managers learn to bury their egos. You are just another gear in the project, but what a big gear! Or maybe the motor or engine that runs the big gear. This is where you to demonstrate and show the people in your company your value and explain to them your role. Once they see your value then they become a believer in project management.

This is where you to demonstrate and show the people in your company your value and explain to them your role. Once they see your value then they become a believer in project management.

Heading into Trouble

Trouble is part of being a Project Manager. Once you see you are heading into trouble, you need to take corrective action immediately. Trouble can be many things, cost, schedule, quality, and technical failure, among others. The first thing to do is to alert your boss, the team and the Product Engineer or Business Marketing Manager or whoever reports to the customer. I have a rule: "bad news does not get better over time" so I alert my boss or whoever needs to know immediately. The Project

Manager will need to figure out what corrective action is needed to get back to homeostasis.

You need to develop a corrective action plan so you can monitor the situation and report status on the issue.

Real Life Stories

Here are some real life stories that happened to me. I am writing them down because you may be able to learn from them or commiserate with me on similar things that have happened to you.

A Boss Who Didn't Like Me

I once had a boss who didn't like me because his boss hired me, but I worked my tail off to show him my worth.

I returned from an overseas assignment with Hughes Aircraft Company and the company allowed me time to find a new job. It seemed liked it was time for me to try and advance myself from Field Engineer to a higher management position. I interviewed with the Director of a Design Manufacturing department. It took some convincing to help the Director understand that I would make a good Project Engineer. He decided to give me the position. I received my start date and reported to the location where I would be working. We were designing a laser rangefinder for the new TOW helicopter for the Army. I was assigned to a Section Manager named Pete. It turned out that Pete didn't like me from the start. He didn't take to me because, as I later understood, he never got to interview me for the job. Working for a boss who didn't like me put me in a tough position. I took it as a challenge and showed him I was worthy of the position and that I could do it, but we never quite seemed to warm up to each other. Through another Manager, I learned that a Project Manager in Logistics Engineering was needed in another location and it was a better opportunity that pulled me away from Pete. I was happy to go to a more pleasant spot.

Getting Bought by Broadcom

I work for a premier RF semiconductor chip making company and we had an office in Irvine, CA. The company's headquarters was in southeast United States. We won a major contract to make a GPS chip for a Nokia cell phone. We were doing well and made it through where Nokia was starting to buy thousands of samples from us though headquarters wanted to make a change and sell the department. We all worked on edge but the company asked us not to leave promising that after the department was acquired we would receive 50% of our salary for staying on. We all thought this was a good deal and we all decided to stay on. Of course, knowing what companies are like these days, I decided to polish up my resume anyway and had it ready to go at a moment's notice.

Suitors started to show up and visit our plant. One day we recognized the people that came as being from Broadcom. It seemed Broadcom was going to buy us. Then, on July 15 it was announced there would be an all-hands meeting. The scuttlebutt was that a Broadcom VP was coming to announce they were buying us. We all assembled in the meeting area feeling a bit euphoric thinking the Vice President of Broadcom was coming to announce that they bought us. Then, the Director stood up and introduced our company's VP from Human Resources and he announced that we were all laid off and the facility was closing. Wow! The air was knocked out of us and you could hear a pin drop. We asked what happened to the offer that was made from the first suitor that was turned down. Why didn't our company accept that? There was nothing more to say; we were all laid off without the 50% of our salary offer-just the sharp pin prick to the heart. Now it turned out Broadcom became the winner of this deal as they cherry picked from the available people and hired them. They won without investing a dime.

Ralph Turbo - Silver Tongued Devil

I once had a boss who could sell the Brooklyn Bridge. He was the smoothest and quickest talker I ever knew. He could think on his feet extremely quickly in real time. He said things that would make your head spin. He was such a good talker. He knew how to persuade and sell ideas like I never saw before. He was better than any politician I have ever heard. It was a pleasure listening to him, because you would ask yourself, "How does a person think so quickly on his feet with such compelling answers?" I labeled him the silver-tongued devil because he could talk so eloquently and persuasively.

A Boss Who Believes in Promotions and Raises

Murray Hoffman taught us to give more not less. As a Project Engineer, I was at the lowest level of management in aerospace. I went to work for Murray and I found out Murray believed in two things: promotions and raises for his people. Wow, we should have more people like him! I thought it would take me five years before I could become a Senior Project Engineer. Murray promoted me in one. Yes, I must have shown him something, but what Murray got from me from then on was great loyalty. He also managed to get me a higher raise then I expected. There is nothing like having a boss who really looks out for you. What you then provide him is trust and loyalty and you have his back as he has yours.

Show That You Care

When I did a "Lessons Learned" meeting at the end of a project, I always received high marks from the team for showing them that I cared. You always need to show your team that you care. Below is a true story that demonstrates this and I did not even know it at the time.

When we were building the Magellan GPS Vehicle Navigation for automobiles, I thought the team could use some refreshments in the afternoon. After receiving permission from my boss, I decided to bring in refreshments at 3:00 PM in the afternoon on Wednesdays and Fridays. At first I brought cookies, soda and a big plate of fruit from Sam's Club that cost $40. As time went on the team liked the fruit the most and said that was what they wanted. It wasn't a big deal at $40 a pop twice a week to refresh the team. When we did the Lessons Learned meeting at the end of the project, however, the fruit was the #3 item the team said they liked the best. I asked them why, not knowing why they would say such a thing. Well, they said, we liked it because it showed you care. Wow! I thought that was amazing and something I never thought about.

Now here's a humorous side to me bringing in the fruit. There was this one lady, Jill, who would come up to me and say, "David, the strawberries aren't red enough! Or the blueberries aren't blue enough!" This made me smile, thinking you can't always please everyone. But I responded by telling her, "But they're *free*!"

There are other ways to show people you care. I had a boss at Printrak that used to give out a $25 gift certificate to Chili's restaurant and two movie tickets. I thought that was very nice, but my wife thought it was extremely nice. She said, "Wow, I do not need to cook dinner and we can go to a movie." As someone once told me: 'happy wife, happy life.'

Also I learned to bring in donuts or bagels or something nice on occasion to show you care.

Also tell the team…"Be proud of yourselves. We have accomplished something greater than any single accomplishment. **We** are a **team**!"

Do Things That Others Don't Want to Do...Sweep the Floor

I have a rule that I will do what other people prefer not to do. If I need to make coffee or throw out the trash, I will do it. I show the team that I, too, am part of team and I will do what it takes. It is not beneath me to do menial jobs. After I am done with a meeting, I will straighten up the room, push the chairs-in, straighten up the desk, and throw out the cups people left behind. If I use the last cup of coffee, I make a new pot. Believe the office is an extension of your own house. There is nothing worse than going for a cup a coffee and finding that someone used it up and did not make another pot.

Let's get dirty. There nothing like doing what ten other people need to do. What I mean by this is, after my tenure as a Project Manager contractor was completed, I kept in contact with the people where I worked. They said they needed ten people to do what I did. This was interesting because what I did was the jobs engineers and technical designers didn't want to do because it used up their precious time. I took the load off of them to get the important engineering design work done and not have them worry about the more mundane administrative stuff.

The Stuff That Makes Your Character

Emotional Intelligence

So what is all this Emotional Intelligence about? It popped-up a few years ago. Simply put, Emotional Intelligence is understanding people and why they do things. Why do you do what you do? Why do you have emotions? Where do they come from? Some people are introverts and others are extroverts. Why do they do what they do? Some people think slowly and methodically while others think fast and impulsively to get things done quickly. How do you deal with each one of these different thinking people? Remember, all emotion comes from that part of the brain called the amygdala. The amygdala is where all emotions reside in your brain. Remember: the human body has adapted over four million years and has gone through changes. We use our five senses in a fraction of a second to think about things.

Every day people would come up to me and bombard me with questions about conflicts they are having. They need or want answers. I learned to handle most situations by taking a deep breath and thinking for a second about what is the best answer for the project. I am also not the greatest person for giving fast answers. I sometimes think of this as a knee-jerk reaction. I like to think about it the question for 24 hours, if I have the time. Then, I am able to give a much more informed and thought out answer.

Know Your Strengths and Weaknesses

Self-awareness - "know thyself:" having a self-understanding of one's emotions, strengths, weakness, needs, and drive. Self-aware job candidates will be frank in admitting failure and will often tell their tales with a smile. On my bad days or days that didn't go well, I say "I should have been a plumber." My Grandfather owned a major plumbing company in New York City and he wanted me to take over the business. I told my Grandfather I did not want to. I used to work with my father who was a master plumber and Forman for my Grandfather on Christmas, Easter and during summer vacations. I learned I did not want to deal with the politicians and the unions and other criminal activity.

What are you good or strong at? What are your weaknesses or where do you need improvement? You need to know your strengths so you can use them to gain advantage over all the constraints, obstacles and issues you will face in the work place. Knowing yourself will help you relate to others and be a better person.

My strengths are that I am persistent and determined. I have a lot of energy or zeal to bring to the workplace. I also have presence. How do I know? I found out through my Toastmasters experience. After I gave my first speech someone told me that I have good presence - something I didn't know. I also like to see things in writing as I am a visual person. Some people are auditory. This is a good thing; auditory people want to hear what you say and not write it down. My mind is thinking about many things all the time and darting from one thing to another. I really need to focus on what you are saying when you speak to me or my mind wanders and about 20 seconds later I forgot what you said. But if I write it down, then I have something to look out and remind myself what you said and what needs to be done.

What are your weaknesses? I learned that if someone disrespects me that pushes my button and I get upset. I may say something I wish I didn't later on.

I was not the most technically knowledgeable person in engineering. I didn't always understand what other engineers were talking about in their design work or how it operated. I was just good enough to get by. I have good people skills. Understanding the design would help me understand how the product that needed to be designed and built worked. Using my people skills made me a good Project Manager.

Learning enough of the technical information helped me, but I always tried to improve my technical skills. This amplified my skills overall.

Trust

So what value do you bring to being a Project Manager, to your team and to your peers? What's all this trust stuff about? Why do you need trust?

Without trust you have nothing.

Trust is the one thing that a Project Manager needs. If your people do not trust you, they will not deal with you, nor will they want to deal with you. It was critical to me that if I told you I was going to do something, I did it-no ifs, ands or buts. However, if there was some reason I could not do it such as the boss saying I couldn't or some factor that prevented me, I would find you and tell you why I couldn't do it.

You need to figure out the ways that people can trust you. It is not only your words, but more importantly, your actions.

Ethics and Values

Sometimes you get into a situation where your ethics and values are tested. What I learned is to stay on the high road and not let yourself get caught in a trap. Sometimes this is difficult, because customers, bosses, salespeople and events can get you into this trap unwittingly.

Ethics are the right things to do. Sometimes companies want you to take shortcuts or tell customers half- truths or false information to keep the company or you out of trouble.

The biggest incident I had with ethics was when I was a twenty-five year old and had a job overseas with the military in a foreign country. I worked for an aerospace company teaching the foreign military how to repair high-performance airplanes. The foreign students who attended the classes were very lazy and did not do their work to learn what they really needed to know. However, their advancement was based on their successfully completing the course in a certain amount of time.

When it was time for me to sign-off on their successfully completing the course, I refused to do it. This created a major incident between my boss and the Training Commander who ran the foreign military's teaching department. My boss ordered me to sign off their work. I refused to do so, but told my boss that I had no problem if he or someone else wanted to sign them off, but I couldn't because these students could not competently repair high-performance airplanes.

This issue escalated very quickly to our onsite senior director and chief of the Air Force base of the aerospace company and to a General in the country's military. The aerospace chief finally agreed with me and said we would not sign it off. This led to my being asked to leave the country by the foreign country's Training Commander. He did not want to lose face or look bad, but I spoke with the managers at the base and told them I was competent to work in the field service department on the base where we actually repaired the major navigation systems for the foreign military's high performance airplanes. Consequently, I was reassigned to the Field Engineering slot and stayed in the country.

What was interesting was that no one wanted look bad over this incident. I received a written commendation for my fine work from both the foreign military Training Commander and from the aerospace Air Force base senior director.

You see, I stuck to what I believed in with my ethics intact and received high commendations for it. Go figure!

The lesson learned is to stick to what you believe in and don't let the forces of business get you down. As we know, perception is what others see you as and your character is who and what you are. Believe in your character.

Conflict

Here are some things to consider when it comes to conflict: Sun Tzu, Art of War:

1. What is the science of strategy in conflict? I previously said strategy is how we/you are going to achieve our objectives. Conflict is when you disagree about something or a collision or struggle with an opposite position or opinion.
   Put the two together and you have to come up with method or process on how you will deal with conflict. If a barrier is created how will you deal with it? What is your strategy to deal with conflict?

2. Make conflict altogether unnecessary. Try not to get yourself into conflict situations.

3. Learn to take conflict out of your life. This is hard but think about how, if possible, to avoid conflict.

4. The perk of efficiency of knowledge and strategy is to make conflict altogether unnecessary "to overcome others without fighting is the best of skill."

5. Understanding conflict can lead not only to its resolution, but even to its avoidance altogether.

6. This applies to competition and conflict on every level from interpersonal to international.

7. The aim of avoiding conflict is invincibility, victory without battle and unassailable strength throughout, understanding, physics, politics, business and psychology.

8. A tool for understanding the very root cause of conflict is to learn how to Adapt, Improvise and Overcome.

Dealing with Conflict

- As I said, there will be differences of opinion. You have to listen to these opinions and make the best decision for the project - not for the person or for you.
- To prevent conflict, people must understand the goals and objectives of each project. This may sound like motherhood, but you better be sure for if you assume they do, they probably don't.
- One of the biggest conflicts can be the culture of the company. I am a bit of a risk taker. Some companies are very risk-avoidant and can conflict with your style. The culture sometimes prevents forward movement. What do you do if it is an impediment to your project? I followed their orders; you need to figure out a happy medium to get forward movement. Follow their orders, but don't let the company trifle with your project.
- To avoid conflict establish common priorities, foster a unified sense of purpose and improve collaboration between matrix skill centers and your team.
- Urgent - Feels like it has to be done…It has to be done.
- Important - has to be done or else there are consequences.
- Do you have a solution or a suggestion?

Helpful Sayings When Dealing With People

No People No Problem!

The more I deal with people the better I like my dog.

I make a Difference.

You make a Difference.

We all make a Difference.

Together we make a Difference.

Be proud of yourself. We have accomplished something greater than any singular accomplishment. We are a TEAM! The whole is more than the sum of its parts.

<u>People</u>

Powerful
Popular
Perfect
Peaceful

Dealing with People and Going from Good to Superior

Organize, Manage, and Lead People Teams

You know, it is really hard dealing with people. It is the hardest thing you will ever do! I have a saying: "You think putting on a man on Mars is hard . . . try dealing with relationships!" People are a hard to deal with because each one of us is hard-wired differently and we see the world differently. As a Project Manager, however, how are you going to deal with these differences to organize, work with and get the best from each person on the team? It takes fortitude and understanding to figure out what each person is all about and how they work. Also people work at different levels. What I mean by this is we work at one level to meet the objectives of our projects; our bosses work at a different level to fit the bigger pieces of the puzzle together. Then, their bosses work at an even higher level to fit all the pieces of the puzzle together.

What are the project management fundamentals we must know and deal with? Here is a small list of the characteristics, roles, and functions a Project Manager uses when working and dealing with people:

1. **Role Integrator** – As a role integrator, the Project Manager determines how to get all the people in different roles of the projects(s) to work together.

2. **Speaker and Communicator** - We need to be good communicators. If you can't communicate well you have a high chance of failing.

3. **Leader of People and Teams** - Remember you are the leader: explain how you want people to follow you; why should they follow you and what makes you a good person to follow.

4. **Team Facilitator** – The team facilitator gets tasks to move at the proper rate and keeps everything moving along. When needed during the monitor and control phases, how are you going to "turn the herd" or "organize the cats to work in a cohesive effort?"

5. **Decision Producer and Maker** – The Project Manager makes the decisions for the team and identifies the methods used to make the decisions. These decisions can be hard ones such as firing or replacing someone who is not pulling their weight or getting things done, or is acting as an impediment and preventing the project from moving forward.

6. **Team Builder** – The Project Manager must be able to build the team into one cohesive working unit.

7. **Team Champion** – As Project Manager, you are the champion of the team. You need to be an optimist and tell stakeholders outside of your team how well the team is working together. Remember you represent the team.

8. **Meets the Needs of the Team** – The Project Manager must work to meet the needs of the team, getting them what they need and when they need it.

9. **Supports Overcoming Obstacles** - How are you going to overcome obstacles and constraints of your team. You will need to give great thought on what tactics you will use.

10. **Honest Broker** - An honest broker takes no sides in a dispute or argument and decides what works best to meet the project goals while satisfying the scope, team, and stakeholder needs. The honest broker takes the fear out and assures everyone that "everything is okay."

Employee Relations & Building Relationships

What Makes a Project Manager Succeed in the Real World?

1. **Are you adaptive to the situation?** - Can you adapt, improvise, and overcome any situation that you may face?

2. **Are you organized and structured?** – Working with some form of order will make you more efficient. Color coding of folders is one way. For example, when I see a colored folder on my desk, I know which project it is or what subject it is involves. How do you keep your files and reference books? Are the files on your computer well-organized, orderly, and easy to find?

3. **Can you state your vision** on where you aim to go or be, describe the project mission, and what makes our team different?

4. **Can you deal with people well?** Remember every person is different and how you will deal with each individual to get the best out of them.

5. **Can you bury your ego?** Good project Managers do. Remember, the project is a team effort. Show the team your humility.

6. **Are you are good strategist and tactician?** Do you think creatively? You will need to develop ways to get things done that are beyond your normal methods. They call this "thinking out of the box."

7. **Can you give team members the desire to do their jobs?**

What Distinguishes a Great Project Manager from a Good Project Manager?

1. Believing failure is not an option. Never, never ever giving up.

2. The ability to create solutions with no guidance or budget.

3. The ability to handle ambiguity, deal with the unknowns, and still succeed.

4. An insatiable desire and uncanny ability to learn and get better.

5. The ability to analyze.

6. Patience and stability.

7. Determination and persistence.

Ten Things I Learned from Rick Klemm

1. **Bad news does not get better with time.**

I have always insisted that my team member tell me any bad news right away as soon as it has happened. The reason for this is that I might have time to fix it. I have always asked my team to give me reaction time. Perhaps the problem can be lumped in with other things that need fixing. If the problem is lumped in with other things, then maybe it's not as noticeable as the other items that have been found. Also, you may be able to make a decision and a solution on the problem today, but by tomorrow the issue may have grown and become so big that there is nothing you can do about it.

2. **Let me check the project plan to understand the ripple effect of this issue.**

There is usually a ripple effect when something goes wrong. You plug the delay into your Microsoft Project scheduling plan and you can see how it ripples through your project. Will it extend the end date? In other words, how big of an issue is this?

3. I need some help.

There is nothing wrong with asking for help when you need it. Help could come from management or from your team. I always ask my team two questions at the beginning of a project: 1) What is in your way? 2) What road blocks do you have? Maybe I can help get the road blocks or obstacles out of the way. Just as you asked your team, you need to ask yourself about what is preventing you from moving forward and if you need help removing obstacles.

4. What are the data and facts regarding the issue?

The data is the data, but how the data is interpreted is always an issue. While you might think the data is good enough, your Quality Engineer may disagree. You need to look at the data and the issues you have and determine if the information you have is good enough for the success of the project. If it is, move forward. There is no reason to use up extra time to gold plate the project. That's not what the customer or sponsor paid for.

5. Trust but verify.

This is an old Ronald Reagan saying. Just because a trusted authority said it happened, there is nothing wrong with verifying yourself that it did indeed happen. Remember, when you speak your words should be impeccable.

6. Let me explain why this is important to our customers.

Sometimes by speaking directly with the Business Product Manager (or Marketing Manager, Product Line Manager, or Sales Manager) I have found out what is really important to the customer and why he wants what he wants.

It is important that you communicate to your team what you have found out and even more important why the customer wants it. Your team / people like and need to know what is important to the customer so they can add it to that part of the scope of work that they are responsible for.

7. What can we do now, to prevent a problem in the future?

As the Project Manager you are not the only one who needs to look at risk in the future. The whole team needs to be looking at potential problems in their path. At the beginning of the project during initiation and planning, I always ask the project team what is in their way. What hurdles do they see that potentially may occur? This provides me with the opportunity to maybe solve problems early on in the project. It may mean buying them a piece of software or hardware to make their job easier. Pay some now can result in a big payoff later. It can shorten the project schedule or lower your cost.

8. Don't tell me why it can't be done; tell me what it would take to get it done.

There are people on your team who are always telling you why they can't get it done. I immediately take their thrust, turn it around, and ask what it will take to get it done. Never walk into another person's office and tell them why something cannot be done; always come with options on how the problem can be mitigated. This is where Project Managers must be positive and not negative. I remember going to my boss at Magellan when I had an issue and I came with two suggestions on how to solve it. My boss was wonderful at coming up with a third suggestion that would work just as well. It was kind of a brain storming session where we worked out the issues together - great collaboration.

9. Let's prioritize our key issues.

It is important to prioritize your key issues and work on these first. Prioritize the issues into categories, such as:

- **Urgent:** Must haves or you may not have a project
- **Important:** Has to be done or else there are consequences.
- **Nice to haves:** Things that are nice to do
- **Least important:** Not important and what I call below the line in the scope of work

This way, you can put most of your effort and energy into accomplishing the most urgent important or vital items.

10. A little paranoia is a good thing.

A little paranoia on a project is a good thing. It helps you to keep you sharp and paying attention to what may or could go wrong. It keeps you thinking about what you are responsible for on the project. A great Project Manager will continually verify that all is well and going as smooth as possible, and identity any potential issues early on - especially the ones that can bite you hard!

Dealing with People Who Drive Me Crazy - From the Leadership Freak

The crazy thing about people who make us crazy is that we learn from them. We learn either that it is something worth learning or that they are just a bunch of hot air that will get us nowhere to make project better:

1. Annoying people make you stronger.

2. You learn how to stop them annoying you.

3. You might see a little of yourself in them. Boy isn't that annoying!

4. Grit - You will learn about resistance and how to deal with it - Grit

5. Compassion - Do I annoy more people than I realize.

6. You learn how to stay strong.

7. You Learn how to use Emotional Intelligence with annoying people and not knee jerk reactions.

8. You learn how to tolerate all types of people.

9. You learn how to focus in spite of annoying people who may try to defocus you.

Summary

As you can see this book has been about dealing with real-life situations as a Project Manager. I spoke about the soft skills that you need to know to be a superior Project Manager. In my mind soft skills are more important than the hard skills. While you need to know the hard skills, the soft skills get you ahead in life. How will you cope and survive in the PM jungle?

Well, I wrote about many things. These are hard things, not easy things to wrap your arms around. It will take many years of practice to figure what works and what doesn't work for you. However, I put my forty years of experience into this book to help you to think and determine what actions you choose to take to be a top-notch Project Manager.

Good luck and hang in there with determination, fortitude, zeal, and passion.

**A Noble Profession…Not Easy, But Worth It…
Something Worth It Doesn't Come Easy.**

www.ingramcontent.com/pod-product-compliance
Lightning Source LLC
Chambersburg PA
CBHW021038180526
45163CB00005B/2178